# Pronounce Māori with Confidence

*An Easy Guide – with CD-ROM*

## Hoani Niwa

RAUPO

*To my daughter Muna, on the completion of her course in Te Reo Māori at Hoani Waititi Marae, Waitākere City.*

*Ka nui te mihi atu ki a koe, ka nui te aroha. Hokia ki tōu maunga tupuna kia purea koe e ngā hau o Tāwhirimātea*

A RAUPO BOOK
Published by the Penguin Group
Penguin Group (NZ), 67 Apollo Drive, Rosedale,
North Shore 0632, New Zealand (a division of Pearson New Zealand Ltd)
Penguin Group (USA) Inc., 375 Hudson Street,
New York, New York 10014, USA
Penguin Group (Canada), 90 Eglinton Avenue East, Suite 700, Toronto,
Ontario, M4P 2Y3, Canada (a division of Pearson Penguin Canada Inc.)
Penguin Books Ltd, 80 Strand, London, WC2R 0RL, England
Penguin Ireland, 25 St Stephen's Green,
Dublin 2, Ireland (a division of Penguin Books Ltd)
Penguin Group (Australia), 250 Camberwell Road, Camberwell,
Victoria 3124, Australia (a division of Pearson Australia Group Pty Ltd)
Penguin Books India Pvt Ltd, 11, Community Centre,
Panchsheel Park, New Delhi – 110 017, India
Penguin Books (South Africa) (Pty) Ltd, 24 Sturdee Avenue,
Rosebank, Johannesburg 2196, South Africa

Penguin Books Ltd, Registered Offices: 80 Strand, London, WC2R 0RL, England

First published by Reed Publishing (NZ) Ltd 2003
Reprinted 2004, 2005, 2007

First published by Penguin Group (NZ) 2009
7  9  10  8

Copyright © Hoani Niwa 2003

Printed in China through Asia Pacific Offset
Cover and text designed by Serena Kearns
Illustrations by Muna Niwa
Edited by Graham Wiremu & Peter Dowling

ISBN: 978 0 14 320238 7

A catalogue record for this book is available
from the National Library of New Zealand.

www.penguin.co.nz

# Contents

# Forewords

Learning a new language always presents challenges — and those challenges are especially exciting when the language is unique to one's own country. Suddenly, the stories behind the place names, people and culture we have grown up with come to life, with new contexts and meanings. We discover a treasure trove of history and legend, with language being the key to the casket.

Many New Zealanders, however, find themselves at a disadvantage when learning Māori language. They must rectify a lifetime of bad habits by 'unlearning' incorrect pronunciation of words. Even the word Māori must be relearned, not to mention place names and greetings.

In Pronounce Māori with Confidence, Hoani Niwa recognises these challenges, and guides the student through the basics of pronunciation in a manner that is both instructive and non-threatening. The accompanying CD-Rom reassures the learner that he or she is succeeding.

As a people, we have recognised that the Māori language is a taonga. Our commitment to our beautiful native language is strong. Thanks to Hoani Niwa and others willing to share their knowledge, we can all play a part in ensuring it is nurtured and grown for future generations of New Zealanders.

Mā te kōrero ka ora te reo — speaking will give life to the language.

**The Honourable Dame Silvia Cartwright PCNZM, DBE**
**Governor-General of New Zealand**

It is high time that New Zealanders learn to pronounce the Māori language correctly.

A language is a window to a culture and a nation. To respect the language is to respect the culture. Here in Aotearoa our Māori language is special. It is the indigenous language of the country and also the official language of New Zealanders as confirmed in the 1987 Māori Language Act. It follows that as a nation we ought to be trying to preserve the linguistic integrity of our very own indigenous language. This is consistent with international protocols that recognise access to one's language as a human right.

It is also about relationships and respect for each other's cultures. In a constitutional sense it relates to the language as a taonga of the Māori people. At a community level language provides a basis for effective communication. More and more New Zealanders, both Māori and non-Māori, are learning to speak Māori. This phenomenon will result in an even stronger Māori language presence throughout New Zealand communities.

This Māori language resource is a credit to all involved. It shows leadership and vision. It engenders respect for each other's cultures and provides an excellent learning tool that can be utilised by every New Zealand household.

Mā te reo o tēnā o tēnā ka ora ai 'Te Katoa' — via the synergy of languages the populace will prosper.

**Haami Piripi**
**Chief Executive Officer**
**Te Taura Whiri i te reo Māori/Māori Language Commission**

Hoani Niwa has played an important role for Citizens Advice Bureaux (CAB) in New Zealand in gently supporting and encouraging our efforts to work within the spirit of the Treaty of Waitangi and to make our service accessible and relevant to Māori. As our national kaumātua Hoani has acted as advisor, sounding board and representative on Māoritanga, tikanga, and kawa. Hoani's contribution has also extended to supporting CAB with resources to assist us with Māori pronunciation, and it is a delight to see his passion and expertise expressed in this publication.

Pronounce Maori with Confidence is an important resource for people in Aotearoa/New Zealand, as the use of Māori words and language becomes more and more an everyday event. Hoani's simple but comprehensive approach can be of great use to us all.

Hoani has also generously committed the profits he derives from this book to CAB to support our ongoing bicultural work.

I am delighted to endorse this valuable publication.

**Nick Toonen**
**Chief Executive**
**New Zealand Association of Citizens Advice Bureaux**

## Note

- The macron over a letter (e.g. ā) indicates a long vowel. This is explained on page 14.
- Standard Māori spelling and pronunciation are used in this short course. There are regional variations, particularly in Northland/Te Tai Tokerau, Taranaki and the South Island/Te Wai Pounamu.

# Preface — He mihi

Whāia te iti kahurangi
Ki te tuoho koe
Me he maunga teitei

Seek the treasures of your heart
If you bow your head
Let it be to a lofty mountain

Pronounce Māori with Confidence is the result of many years of close contact with a range of diverse cultures within the community, through my work in the New Zealand Army and statutory and voluntary organisations, such as the Citizens Advice Bureaux/Ngā Pokapū Whakahoki Pātai mai i te Iwi Whānui. The Citizens Advice Bureaux relies totally on communication to carry out its advisory role to people. Through my work it has become obvious to me that the general public, including minority groups and the many ethnicities, are endeavouring to improve their vocabulary and pronunciation skills.

Te reo Māori (the Māori language) permeates all our lives — for example, in place names, personal names and the names of many of our native flora. So even non-speakers of the language need to use Māori words on a day-to-day basis. This book and its accompanying CD-ROM provide an opportunity to understand and learn Māori pronunciation, and at the same time to learn a little of the language to help enable you to converse with people in everyday life.

Written Māori differs from written English. The writing, pronunciation and spelling of English has evolved over centuries and the language is full of irregularities. With Māori, on the other hand, the spelling system was deliberately devised to be consistent, accurate and easy. There are very few rules, and if you learn them and stick to them then it's just a matter of practice to get your tongue around a few sounds which may at first seem difficult. But persevere and you'll find Māori words easy to say.

You should find this book useful — but make sure you read it in conjunction with the CD. This functions as an audio CD, or as a CD-ROM for study on the computer, with the book viewable as an Acrobat PDF file. Listening and speaking are vital, so it's important to play the CD a track at a time and practise aloud, repeating what you have heard. Links from the book to the CD are shown throughout the book. Ideally you will practise with a friend or family member — you will both improve more quickly with someone else there to correct and encourage you.

Māori is an official language of New Zealand and receives growing respect. My hope is that this book and CD package will enhance that respect and benefit everyone in Aotearoa New Zealand's multi-cultural society. If in some way you find new enjoyment and value in what this package offers, you will have gone a long way to reinforcing the cultural diversity and strength of our country.

Here is a whakataukī, a Māori saying, to carry through your practice. It goes like this:

Ko tēnei pukapuka kōpaepae pūoru
He iti e tārei ko māpihi
O te pounamu heitiki, āe
E iti noa e hoatu ngā aroha.

This compact disk book
Small indeed, but shaped for personal adornment
Like a greenstone tiki, yes
A small gift given in love.

## Acknowledgements

There are many people who have contributed to making this book and CD possible. I am especially grateful to Peter Dowling of Reed Publishing for his patience and expertise in bringing the project to fruition. Graham Wiremu provided valuable editorial guidance and support, and the proofreading by Jane McRae, Ross Calman and Mikaera Nepia was much appreciated. Serena Kearns has created a warm and inviting design. Stephanie Martin, Rikihana Smallman, John Haynes and Tamati Te Nohotu were a great team to work with in recording the audio CD. My thanks to Her Excellency the Governor General Dame Silvia Cartwright, Haami Piripi and Nick Toonen for their endorsements. To the many others who have lent encouragement and support, my thanks.

# Pronunciation and the alphabet

Although the Māori language uses the same alphabet as English, there are important differences in the number of letters used and the way some of them are pronounced.

All the sounds in Māori are represented by just 13 letters of the alphabet and two digraphs:

**The 13 letters are:**

Five vowels – **a e i o u**

Eight consonants – **h k m n p r t w**

Two consonants are denoted by digraphs – **wh  ng**

Let's look at each group in turn and discover how to pronounce the individual sounds correctly.

# The vowels

It's the vowels that cause the most trouble for newcomers to Māori, because in English, each vowel can be pronounced in various ways. For example:

| | |
|---|---|
| **a** | pat, past, paste |
| **e** | get, complete, fete |
| **i** | sin, sign |
| **o** | rover, mover, lover, hover |
| **u** | pun, put, repute |

No wonder the vowels cause concern for newcomers to Māori! But there should be no confusion in Māori. It's much simpler and more consistent than in English. You won't go wrong if you remember the following three rules.

# Vowel rule 1

For each of the five vowels there is one sound only.

| | |
|---|---|
| **a** | 'ah' as in 'car' – never as in 'cat' or 'cake' |
| **e** | 'e' as in 'pet' – never as in 'pea' or 'pay' |
| **i** | 'ee' as in 'me' – never as in 'my' |
| **o** | 'aw' as in 'awesome' – never as in 'over' |
| **u** | 'oo' as in 'moon' – never as in 'pure' |

Let's play the CD, listen to these vowel sounds and practise them. Once you've got the hang of these five sounds, you've overcome the biggest stumbling block to pronouncing Māori correctly and confidently.

|   | A | E | I | O | U |
|---|---|---|---|---|---|
| A | a-a | a-e | a-i | a-o | a-u |
| E | e-a | e-e | e-i | e-o | e-u |
| I | i-a | i-e | i-i | i-o | i-u |
| O | o-a | o-e | o-i | o-o | o-u |
| U | u-a | u-e | u-i | u-o | u-u |

## Vowel rule 2

**The vowel sound can be said quickly (a short vowel) or more slowly (a long vowel).**

A long vowel is not pronounced differently from the short vowel: you simply linger on it as you say it.

Long vowels are indicated either by doubling the letter – **aa ee ii oo uu** – or by using a macron over the letter – **ā ē ī ō ū**. The macron system is increasingly common today, and is the system used in this book.

Even with macrons, you will still see the occasional double vowel – as in words like 'Mātaatua'(one of the first canoes) and 'ātaahua'(attractive), which has both a macron and a double vowel! The reason is that in these cases the word is a compound – of 'mata' and 'ātua', and 'āta'and 'āhua'.

When you see double vowels, avoid the temptation to pronounce them as you would in English. For example, 'Te Kooti'does not rhyme with 'booty'; it rhymes with 'naughty'.

It's important to make the distinction between long and short vowels, as they can significantly affect the meaning of a word.

For example:

| | |
|---|---|
| **keke** | cake |
| **kekē** | creak |
| **kēkē** | armpit |

or

| | |
|---|---|
| **runa** | ribbonwood |
| **rūna** | earthquake |
| **rūnā** | pull together |

If we go back to the CD we can listen to the way the long vowels sound. Practise saying the short vowels along with the long vowels until the distinction is clear in your mind – and in your pronunciation. Now take a deep breath and here we go:

**a-ā**

**e-ē**

**i-ī**

**o-ō**

**u-ū**

# Vowel rule 3

**When two vowels appear together, each must be pronounced separately.**

In English, when two vowels appear together they often form a new sound altogether. For example:

peat, said, toast, bread, neither

But in Māori, it is important that each vowel is given its own sound. In effect, every vowel is a separate syllable. It is also worth noting that every syllable in Māori ends in a vowel.

It is common to find three or more vowels following each other, and you need to practise saying them all distinctly. To emphasise this point, hyphens have been inserted between the vowels in the following examples. Let's listen to the CD again.

**a-ō**

**ī-u-ē-a**

**ā-ē-ī-o-o**

**u-a-e-ō**

**e-a-ū-o-ī--e**

**ō-i-e-ā-o**

**ē-ū-ā-ō**

**e-ā-ū-o-i-a-ē-e-i-ō-a-e**

**ē-ī-ā-o-e-i-u**

Try these words:

| | |
|---|---|
| **ō-i** | quicksand |
| **Ō-ne-wa** | Northcote (Auckland) |
| | |
| **to-i** | art |
| **tō-ī** | mountain cabbage tree |
| | |
| **nō-nā-i-a-nei** | just now, modern |
| **Tar-i mō Ngā Ta-ke Pū-nga-o** | Ministry of Energy |

# The consonants

The eight consonants are – **h k m n p r t w**

In Māori the consonants are pronounced much as they are in English, with a few exceptions. One exception is the letter **r**, which is never rolled or trilled. Its sound is very close to 'd' or 'l'. When you make these two sounds, notice how you flick your tongue against your palate. To say **r** correctly in Māori, you flick just the tip of your tongue in the same way.

Let's practise saying **r**. You'll find these examples on your CD.

**ra  re  ri  ro  ru**

| | | | Remember vowel rule 1 |
|---|---|---|---|
| **Te Ra-ra-wa** | Te Rarawa | Northland iwi | Te-rah-rah-wah |
| **Re-re-ra-ngi** | Rererangi | Aeroplane | Re-re-rah-ngee |
| **Ri-ri** | Riri | Angry | Ree-ree |
| **Ro-ro-hi-ko** | Rorohiko | Computer | Raw-raw-hee-kaw |
| **Ru-ru** | Ruru | Morepork | Roo-roo |

| | | | |
|---|---|---|---|
| **U-ru-u-ru-ro-ro-a** | Uruururoroa | Dragonfly | Oo-roo-oo-roo-raw-raw-ah |
| **Ra-ru-ra-ru** | Raruraru | Problems | Rah-roo-rah-roo |
| **Ko-rō-ri-a** | Korōria | Glory | Kaw-raw-ree-ah |
| **A-ra-rā!** | Ararā! | Look here | Ah-rah-rah |
| **Re-o I-ri-ra-ngi** | Reo Irirangi | Radio | Re-oo ee-ree-rah-ngee |
| **Mā-rō-rō** | Mārōrō | Strong | Mah-raw-raw |

Another exception is the letter **t**. Listen closely and you'll notice that it sometimes sounds like the 't' in English. This is before an 'i' or a 'u'. But when it comes before an 'a', 'e' or 'o', the sound is softer — almost like a 'd' in English. As with the letter 'r', it's to do with how you place your tongue against the palate.

Let's give **t** a try.

>   **ti tu,**
>   but **ta te to**
>   Again: **ti tu ta te to**

Listen to your CD for examples using **t**.

# The digraphs

The digraphs (double letters) **wh** and **ng** each represent a single consonant.

**Wh** is most commonly pronounced 'f', though the pronunciation varies from region to region. In the north, for example, you will hear 'h' or 'hw'. In Taranaki and Whanganui, they say 'w'. The 'f' sound is universally understood and for a learner it makes sense to stick to it.

You may be wondering: if **wh** is pronounced most commonly as 'f', why isn't it spelt that way? The reason is that when English missionaries and academics first established a system for spelling and writing Māori, they did so with the help of chiefs from Ngā Puhi in Northland. Here they pronounced **wh** as 'hw', the sound many people (Pākehā as well as Māori) still use today when they say 'when', 'wheel' and so on.

The **ng** sound is easy. It is the sound in the middle of 'hanging' and 'singing' – though in Māori you will often find it at the front of a word.

The important thing to remember is that you never pronounce the **g** separately as you do in 'fungus' or 'dingo'.

Practise these words with digraphs:

| Insects | | | Remember vowel rule 1 |
|---|---|---|---|
| **Whē** | Whē | Stick insect | Fay |
| **Wha-re-ngā-ra-ra** | Wharengārara | Parasite | Fah-re-ngah-rah-rah |
| **Nga-nga-ra** | Ngangara | Spider, insect | Ngah-ngah-rah |
| **Ngu-tu-ta-wa** | Ngututawa | Green beetle | Ngoo-too-tah-wah |

| Place names | | | Remember vowel rule 1 |
|---|---|---|---|
| **Whā-ngā-rei** | Whāngārei | Whangarei | Fah-ngah-ray |
| **Wha-nga-pa-rā-o-a** | Whangaparāoa | near Auckland | Fah-ngah-pah-rah-aw-ah |
| **Wha-ka-tā-ne** | Whakatāne | in Bay of Plenty | Fah-kah-tah-ne |
| **Ngo-ngo-ta-hā** | Ngongotahā | near Rotorua | Ngaw-ngaw-tah-hah |
| **Ngā-whā** | Ngāwhā | in Northland | Ngah-fah |
| **Ngā-mo-tu** | Ngāmotu | New Plymouth | Ngah-maw-too |

| Names of flora | | | Remember vowel rule 1 |
|---|---|---|---|
| **Whī-na-u** | Whīnau | Tree | Fee-nah-oo |
| **Whe-u-whe-u** | Wheuwheu | Feather moss | Fee-u-fee-u |
| **Wha-u** | Whau | Cork tree | Fah-oo |
| **Wha-u-whi** | Whauwhi | Lacebark | Fah-oo-fee |
| **Nga-ra-nga-ra** | Ngarangara | Ice plant | Ngah-rah-ngah-rah |
| **Nga-i-o** | Ngaio | Coastal shrub | Ngah-ee-aw |

# Syllables

This table outlines all the two-letter syllables in the language, simply made up of a consonant and a vowel:

|   | A | E | I | O | U |
|---|---|---|---|---|---|
| H | ha | he | hi | ho | hu |
| K | ka | ke | ki | ko | ku |
| M | ma | me | mi | mo | mu |
| N | na | ne | ni | no | nu |
| P | pa | pe | pi | po | pu |
| R | ra | re | ri | ro | ru |
| T | ta | te | ti | to | tu |
| W | wa | we | wi | wo | wu |

Here are some basic expressions using words of one- and two-letter syllables. With practice, you can start to make conversation.

CD TRACK 13

| | | |
|---|---|---|
| **Tē-nā ko-e** | Tēnā koe | Greetings, good day |
| **E pē-he-a a-na ko-e?** | E pēhea ana koe? | How are you? |
| **E pa-i a-na a-u** | E pai ana au | I'm fine |
| **Me ko-e?** | Me koe? | And you? |
| **Ā-e** | Āe | Yes |
| **Kā-o** | Kāo | No |
| **A-ri a-u** | Ari au | Excuse me |
| **Ko wa-i tō ingoa?** | Ko wai tō ingoa? | What's your name? |
| **Ko ___ tōku ingoa** | Ko ___ tōku ingoa | My name is ___ |
| **Kei te ha-ri a-u ki te tū-ta-ki ki a ko-e** | Kei te hari au ki te tūtaki ki a koe | I am pleased to meet you |
| **Ka ki-te a-nō** | Ka kite anō | See you later |

Now here are the three-letter syllables
(remember vowel rule 1):

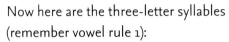

| wh | **wha whe whi who whu** | **fah fe fee faw foo** |
|----|-------------------------|------------------------|
| ng | **nga nge ngi ngo ngu** | **ngah nge ngee ngaw ngoo** |

Let's practise pronouncing words with syllables of one, two and three
letters. Try these words relating to a marae and its activities.

| **To-mo-ka-nga** | Tomokanga | Gate entrance |
|------------------|-----------|---------------|
| **Wha-re-nu-i** | Wharenui | Meeting house |
| **Wha-re-kai** | Wharekai | Dining hall |
| **Wha-i-kō-re-ro** | Whaikōrero | Formal speech-making |
| **Tū-ra-nga-wa-e-wa-e** | Tūrangawaewae | Home ground |
| **Ka-u-mā-tu-a** | Kaumātua | Elders |
| **Wa-i-a-ta** | Waiata | Song |
| **Ma-nu-hi-ri** | Manuhiri | Visitors |
| **Pō-whi-ri** | Pōwhiri | Welcome |
| **Hu-nga ma-te** | Hunga mate | The dead |
| **Hu-nga o-ra** | Hunga ora | The living |
| **Te wha-ka-mu-tu-nga** | Te whakamutunga | The conclusion |
| **Ko-ha** | Koha | Gift |
| **Ho-ngi** | Hongi | Pressing noses |
| **Wha-ka-ta-u-kī** | Whakataukī | Proverb/saying |

Although every syllable and every vowel needs to be said distinctly, you will notice from
the CD that the vowels run smoothly and fluidly from one to the next.

# Stress

By now you should have a pretty good feel for pronouncing the individual syllables that make up words. However, this doesn't mean you will necessarily get the pronunciation of a whole word quite right, because you won't know which syllable or syllables should be stressed. This is important in English too, where a change of emphasis can change the whole meaning of a word. To take just one example:

desert        arid terrain

desert        run away

With many Māori words the incorrect pronunciation is so widespread that you hear it more often than the correct pronunciation. For example, here are some place names as commonly pronounced; following is the correct Māori pronounciation:

| WRONG | RIGHT | |
|-------|-------|---|
| Horowhenua | Horowhenua | Haw-raw-fe-noo-ah |
| Manuka | Mānuka | Mah-noo-kah |
| Otahuhu | Ōtāhuhu | Aw-tah-hoo-hoo |
| Te Kauwhata | Te Kauwhata | Te-kaw-oo-fah-tah |

So how do you know where the stress should fall in a Māori word? There are no easy rules this time, you have to learn as you go. But one clue is that the stress often falls on the first syllable or the first long vowel, as in these examples:

| | |
|---|---|
| Paekākāriki | Henare |
| Ruatāhuna | Renata |
| Ruatōria | Korowhiti |

Since there is no hard and fast rule for stress, it pays to listen well to fluent speakers and identify the areas where you should place emphasis.

# Commonly mispronounced words

CD TRACK 17

As well as place names, many other Māori words have found their way into common usage. While this adds variety and flavour to New Zealand English, the downside is that such words suffer from repeated mispronunciation.

Here are just a few of them:

| | |
|---|---|
| **Māori** | Not maw-ri |
| **Haka** | Not harker |
| **Kauri** | Not kow-ri |
| **Hāngi** | Not hang-y or hang-gy |
| **Kōwhai** | Not koh-eye |
| **Whare** | Not worry |
| **Kahawai** | Not car-why |
| **Pōwhiri** | Not pow-free |

In every case the spelling offers the clues to pronounce the word correctly. Keep in mind the sample pronunciation for the five vowels, as illustrated in Vowel rule 1 on page 12.

# Personal names

It's particularly important to take care with people's names. With what you have now learned, try these, checking with the CD:

| | |
|---|---|
| Hēni | Muna |
| Mere | Hōri |
| Rangi | Ripeka |
| Hēmi | Korotaia |
| Hēnare | Nōpera |
| Katerina | Tāne |
| Rewi | Paikea Ngārangi |
| Rāwiri | Rōpata Tītahi |
| Īhaka | Watino |
| Hone | Witi |
| Renata | Te Whiti |

# At the marae

If you have the opportunity to attend a hui at a marae, it will make your visit more interesting and rewarding if you know the following words – what they mean and how to pronounce them.

| | |
|---|---|
| **Hui** | Gathering, meeting |
| **Tangata whenua** | 'People of the land', the locals |
| **Manuhiri** | Guests, visitors |
| **Ope** | Travelling group |
| **Karanga** | Call of welcome |
| **Wero** | Challenge |
| **Marae** | Open area in front of meeting house; the whole complex of buildings around the marae |
| **Paepae** | Bench or line-up of speech makers |
| **Whaikōrero** | Oratory, speech-making |
| **Mihi** | Greeting |
| **Waiata** | Song or chant |
| **Karakia** | Prayer, prayers |
| **Waka** | Canoe, or descent group from crew of a canoe |

| | |
|---|---|
| **Iwi** | Tribe |
| **Hapū** | Sub-tribe |
| **Whānau** | Family |
| **Whare hui** | Meeting house |
| **Whare whakairo** | Carved house |
| **Wharenui** | Meeting house |
| **Wharekai** | Dining hall |
| **Poupou** | Large posts with carved figures lining the walls of a meeting house |
| **Tukutuku** | Lattice work panels between the poupou |
| **Kōwhaiwhai** | Patterns painted on ceiling rafters |
| **Hākari** | Feast |
| **Poroporoaki** | Speech of farewell |

# More practice

Now let's look at some other categories of Māori words you are likely to come across. They're all good oral practice.

## Iwi (tribes)

Here are the major iwi shown in their respective territories. Practise pronouncing these names with the CD.

Ngāti Kuri

Te Aupōuri

Northern part of the North Island
(Te Hiku a Ika)

Ngāi Takoto

Ngāti Kahu

Te Rarawa

Ngāti Hine

Te Moana Nui A Kiwa

Ngā Puhi

Ngāti Wai

Ngāti Whātua

Ngāti Whātua ki Tāmaki

Ngāti Whanaunga

Ngāti Tai

Ngāti Maru

Te Moana Tāpokapoka a Tāwhaki

Ngāti Te Ata

Ngāti Pāoa

Ngāti Hauā

Ngāti Ranginui

Waikato

Ngāti
Tamaterā
Ngāi Te Rangi

Te Whānau-
a-Apanui

Ngāti Mahuta          Te Arawa          Whakatōhea

Ngāti
Toa          Ngāti          Ngāti          Ngāti
Raukawa          Awa          Porou

Ngāti Maniapoto          Ngāti          Tūhoe          Te Aitanga-a-Hauiti
Tūwharetoa          Te Aitanga-a-Māhaki

Ngāti          Ngāti          Rongowhakaata
Mutunga          Tama          Ngāi Tāmanuhiri

Te Āti Awa          Ngāti          Ngāti Kahungunu
Haua          ki Wairoa          Rongomaiwahine

Taranaki          Ngāti Kahungunu
ki Heretaunga

Ngā Ruahine          Te Āti Haunui-
a-Papārangi

Ngāti Ruanui

Ngā
Rauru

Ngāti Apa

Rangitāne
Muaūpoko
Ngāti Raukawa

Ngāti Toa

Ngāti Kahungunu
Te Āti Awa          ki Wairarapa          Te Moana Nui A Kiwa

North Island (Te Ika a Maui)
below Hamilton

32

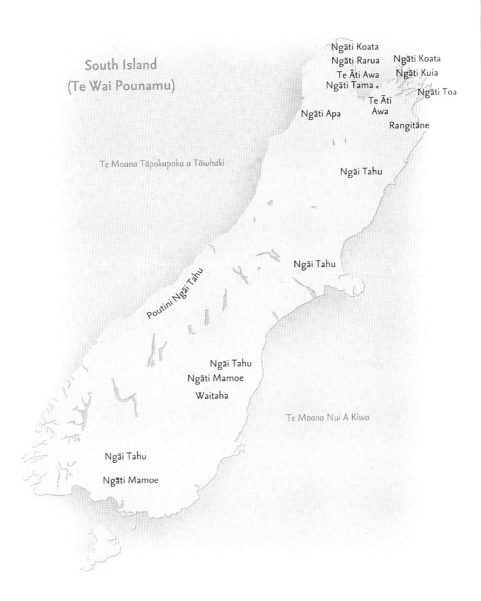

South Island
(Te Wai Pounamu)

Ngāti Koata
Ngāti Rarua    Ngāti Koata
Te Āti Awa    Ngāti Kuia
Ngāti Tama
                    Ngāti Toa
              Te Āti
              Awa
Ngāti Apa
              Rangitāne

Te Moana Tāpokapoka a Tāwhaki

Ngāi Tahu

Ngāi Tahu

Poutini Ngāi Tahu

Ngāi Tahu
Ngāti Mamoe
Waitaha

Te Moana Nui A Kiwa

Ngāi Tahu

Ngāti Mamoe

# Colours

| | |
|---|---|
| **Mangu/pango** | Black |
| **Mā** | White |
| **Whero** | Red |
| **Kōwhai** | Yellow |
| **Parakaraka/ārani** | Orange |
| **Kākāriki** | Green |
| **Kahurangi** | Blue |
| **Kikorangi** | Sky blue |
| **Māwhero** | Pink |
| **Parāone** | Brown |
| **Pūma/kerei** | Grey |

A few macrons in this group. Did you lengthen your vowels?

# Place names

Up till now we have been breaking Māori words down into syllables of one, two and three letters to allow you to distinguish where the vowels are positioned in a word.

Let's try breaking these place names down into one- and two-letter syllables:

| | | |
|---|---|---|
| Ōtira | Ō-ti-ra | Waiau |
| Waimā | | Rāroa |
| Ōtara | | Ōtāne |
| Ōwaka | | Hāwea |
| Ōtākou | | Ōhope |
| Pāhou | | Matea |

Simply find the lone vowel, or separate two vowels that have come together in a word. The remaining four letters are made up of a consonant and a vowel.

**Practise reading these names fluently with the CD.**

Now follow from your CD with some more place names:

| | |
|---|---|
| Waikouaiti | Hungahunga |
| Kaitangata | Awakaponga |
| Taumarunui | Rotomahana |
| Ōtaramarae | Tahorakurī |
| Ngongotahā | Mangatangi |
| Mangawhero | Whangapua |

If you got from four to seven syllables in each word from this last practice, well done.

Now try these longer words:

| | | |
|---|---|---|
| Ōmārama | Aoraki | Paenga |
| Taitapu | Akaroa | Kaikōura |
| Ōamaru | Hokitika | Waimate |
| Tekapō | Harihari | Rangiora |
| Taupō | Wairoa | Tūrangi |
| Rotorua | Ōpōtiki | Tokoroa |
| Katikati | Te Puke | Paeroa |
| Paihia | Hauraki | Hāwera |
| Waiouru | Waitara | Tikorangi |
| Ōeo | Oti | Ite |
| Urenui | Rāhotu | Parihaka |

It's time for some much longer words. But now you've got the hang of breaking a word down into syllables, I'm sure you will find it much easier to say these place names:

CD TRACK 23

| | |
|---|---|
| Hauhungaroa | Tānehopuwai |
| Whangamōmona | Whakarewarewa |
| Poarangitautahi | Tāmaki Makaurau |
| Matemateaonga | Mangatāwhiri |
| Maungaharuru | Maungakiekie |
| Ahimanawa | Maungawhau |
| Mangateretere | Moengawahine |
| Waerengaahika | Mangatoiore |
| Whakaangiangi | Urupukapuka |
| Whangaparāoa | Mimiwhangata |
| Tāwharemānuka | Tangiterōria |
| Tāngarākau | Ngengeroa |

If you're feeling game, here's New Zealand's (and the world's) longest place name:

Taumatawhakatangihangakōauauotamateapōkaiwhenuakitanatahu

# Conclusion — He mihi whakamutunga

By now, many Māori words won't look so forbidding. I hope you will have begun to notice the intrinsic rhythms in other words where once they seemed an impossible mixture of vowels and consonants. If so, you're beginning to develop an ear for the language and I hope you will want to pursue te reo Māori further than this little book can take you.

There are plenty of ways to extend your knowledge. Full-time, part-time, day and evening courses are almost certainly available in your area; ask at a local school or public library. A list of books on Māori language and Māoritanga (culture) appears at the end of this book. Take every opportunity to listen to Māori being spoken – on TV and radio, and among your Māori friends for example. Soon you'll be joining in! If you are invited to visit a marae, seize the opportunity, because here you are likely to hear the language spoken naturally and fluently. You will also hear te reo Māori at its poetic best in the form of whaikōrero, or formal speech-making.

A feature of whaikōrero is the use of whakataukī (proverbs) to highlight a point. We opened with one such saying; here is another whakataukī to end this book.

Pū ana roto
Kē ana waho
Ka pū te ruha
Ka hao te rangatahi
I runga i te mahi aroha.


The positive force is at the centre
The negative force is at the outer shell
The old elements are discarded
And the new elements are created
By the power of love.